All Tito's Children

T0096548

All Tito's Children

Tim Grgec

Victoria University of Wellington Press

Victoria University of Wellington Press
PO Box 600 Wellington
New Zealand
vup.wgtn.ac.nz

A catalogue record is available at the National Library of New Zealand

ISBN 9781776564286

Printed by Markono Print Media Pte Ltd

for Majka and Deda

Contents

Words, as is well known, are the great foes of reality.

—Joseph Conrad

Sometimes what can be invented about a person will tell you quite a lot about him.

—Ivo Andrić

I. The Quarrel with Stalin

To Joseph Stalin,

Stop sending people to kill me! We've already captured five of them, one of them with a bomb and another with a rifle . . . If you don't stop sending killers, I will send a very fast working one to Moscow and I certainly will not have to send another.

JOSIP BROZ TITO
Belgrade, Yugoslavia. Sept. 18, 1948

My people,
is Yugoslav socialism better than Russian? Indeed,
for Yugoslavs only ration milk, bread,
Russians, the spirit. Without Stalin,
our feet will again begin
to feel the ground beneath them—
a snow thawing, clear, like polished spectacles.

The last time I met with Stalin
was at Lake Ritsa for one
of his late-night suppers.

Most on couches and chairs,
some collapsed on the floor,
all were obliged to guess

the temperature outside
and drink a glass of vodka
for every degree they were out.

Stalin then cleared the servants,
our delegates, so it was just he and I
spooning heavy soup

to one another,
warming the loss
of our old Slavic ways.

When I declared myself President on January 14, 1953, I decided the first priority would be a return to truth-telling, that from then two and two would make four and not the solution of Stalin.

'Truth will lead us,' I said, offering spare cigarettes from my military jacket to Belgraders walking leisurely in the parliamentary gardens. With a slow glow on my lips, it was as if I just wandered off one morning; the shadow of the USSR no longer hanging over me, darkening the circles under my eyes.

**Yugoslav Leader Attempts to Liberate Himself
from Freedom**

THE COMMUNIST PARTY of the Soviet Union has
ordered the removal of all state photographs in which
government officials appear in company with Marshal Tito.
According to reports, even his grainy black pictures in old
newspapers will have to be collected, excised. Moscow assures
that these traces of the past will not vanish, but rather bring
another past into view. Officially, the process will be known as
the Recirculation of Blank Spaces, or: the wintry loneliness of
a Yugoslav general headed West.

Pravda, Feb. 20, 1948

II: Elizabeta

In every sitting room, above the Madonna,
a picture of our brave, handsome leader:
Tito in military uniform,
to keep our actual fears away.

As a child, I collected newspaper clippings of Marshal Tito
so I could catch him at every angle, in every light.
I held him, my thumbs ink-stained,
until each impression seemed
no longer his, but mine:
Tito, with broad shoulders, looking stern,
Tito watching the photographer's every move,
Tito in Belgrade
inventing factories and roads.
He even came to me in my dreams, the world
in which I escaped the walnut-brown soil,
and was said in church to be a vision
of eternity.

Perhaps the ink smudged on my fingers was the same as
the dirt on our hands and knees after a day in the fields?
A feeling that goes by unnoticed until you're walking home
in the weakening light, too busy to have noticed the hardness
of the day, rummaging about the earth as our village had
always done.

This was a game my brother and I played in the old country:
each of us took our turn by telling two truths
and one lie about themselves.

If you thought quickly, you could come up with a lie
that was partly true, a half-lie. Of course, the lie was
the easiest part. It was much harder to reveal something
about yourself, even in a game.

1. I left Yugoslavia in 1957, never to return.

2. Your great-grandfather, like everyone else in Međimurje,
    was a basket-maker. He hung willow straws in the sun
    the colour of mottled apples ripening.

3. Back then, I caught chickens with my bare hands.

Stjepan then guessed the lie. We played on the way to church,
or when Majka asked for mushrooms from the edge of
the wood.

Međimurje was once part of Pannonia, a distant province of the Roman Empire, where large trees grew too close together, as if suffocating one another. The Romans feared the birds of the region, birds that were said to have tiny human hands and feet; creatures so extraordinary you would be compelled to follow them into the forest that stretched deep beyond the border: a place that might be another world but could just as easily be hell.

It was not until the Early Middle Ages that we Slavs settled in Međimurje. Its name means 'land surrounded by water'. There was a smell to the earth there. Those from elsewhere did not know it: the smell of silt and sand, enclosed by the Mura, and over there, the Drava. A richness, the soil we dug potatoes from and no grotesque birds to speak of.

Sometimes it was easier to tell truths about someone else, someone long dead reaching forward from the past. Or someone we had never met.

1. Tito made Yugoslavia from melted down Balkan countries

2. Every republic had one town named in Tito's honour. I still remember them now: Titograd (Montenegro), Titov Veles (Macedonia), Titov Drvar (Bosnia and Herzegovina), Titova Korenica (Croatia), Titovo Užice (Serbia) and Titovo Velenje (Slovenia).

3. After his death in 1980, it was revealed Tito was actually a body double, replaced by the Russians during the Second World War.

We whispered stories like these around the village, even though they were forbidden. Tito's name crossed many lips and, after many years, the pictures of him over every blackboard grew real pairs of eyes.

Other times we chose categories.

1. Croatia is the homeland of Marco Polo.

2. It was Ruđer Bošković, Croatian polymath, who suggested building five iron bands on the dome of St Peter's Basilica when a crack was discovered.

3. If you were to spread a map of the world flat, the town of Ludbreg (only 15 miles from Kotoriba) would be exactly in the centre.

Most of these things I learnt from my encyclopaedia—the leather-bound volume I carried with me around the village. With it I felt as if I carried parts of the earth from another time, so that the ground I walked on might not seem so settled. Stjepan and I were always reading. We wanted to know the whole world.

Dear Marshal Tito,

A family secret, the recipe for my baka's chicken soup:

> carrots
> chicken (heart, liver, stomach)
> onion
> parsley, celery
> leaves of cabbage washed white, their pressed white veins
> salt

My baka says this is the secret to her old age. She sighs and shuffles, says you must drink it every day—light-coloured food, after all, is better for you than dark. Years of mincing garlic have gone by her. She stops occasionally to correct the crick in her back and to pass on to me her aching spine.

She says she thinks of you when she lies awake at night. Thankful for how even the old are favoured here in this world of ours, your world, with no need to exaggerate their ailments in order to escape work, unlike those pigs we keep, whom I suspect can hunt and tug as other animals can but prefer to live their lives asleep in the mud.

Each month, with a pencil, she measures the height of my soul on the wall. The sound of her praying, so softly, her voice, she's often misplacing it in the dark.

Sincerely,

Elizabeta Tomasič

Sometimes, if you knew something well, you could come up with three quotes: two true, one made up. The trick was to speak in the style of another person, as if their voice and manner were yours.

As an adolescent, I read and reread Ivo Andrić, the only Yugoslav writer to win the Nobel Prize in Literature. His masterpiece, *The Bridge on the Drina*, is my favourite book:

1. 'Every human generation has its own illusions with regard to civilization; some believe they are taking part in its upsurge, others that they are witnesses of its extinction.'

2. 'We have all sat here, at one time or another, staring past the stream of faces along the concourse, wondering how it was we unravelled the threads of our agrarian destinies, forever the same yet forever tangled in this place like no other.'

3. 'They looked at the paper and saw nothing in those curving lines, but they knew and understood everything, for their geography was in their blood and they felt biologically their picture of the world.'

It never occurred to me that his characters were bound by ink, by paper margins. To me, these were the thoughts of real peasants wandering about the open air, their voice and footsteps as clear to me as if I were actually walking the dusty roads beside them, their Drina running, running always with somewhere to get to.

My brother, Stjepan, preferred quotes about history. He liked reading about things that had actually happened, things that drew a line between the past and present.

Here is Josip Smodlaka, one of the founders of Yugoslavia. Every one of us knew his speeches by heart:

1. 'The Serbs, Croats and Slovenes are descendants of special Slavic tribes, an elsewhere race, who came down from the Carpathian regions during the early centuries of our age and were all of them completely akin to one another.'

2. 'We are all something and someone.'

3. 'Everywhere else in Europe, the dividing line between Greek and Roman churches corresponds to an ethnic demarcation. Not even the Great Schism, which cuts in half our Yugoslav territory, can separate our identity.'

Across the width of our room, Stjepan and I went back and forth. Of course, it was not so much about the quotes you remembered than the small tells of the body: certain habits with your hands, your fingers clasping here and there, gesturing towards a slight hiccup in your words. Stjepan was older than me. My pauses were so familiar to him, my practised composure, the way I grasped each thought.

Our room was unlike any other room. The candle flickering for attention, stretching the shadows of each surface, where the floorboards and walls moved about in the night.

III: Emergence from the Fog

Attention!

Attention!

Belgrade is speaking.

All radio stations of Yugoslavia are broadcasting. Listen to the speech of the Secretary General, the President, our leader, Marshal Tito.

Comrades, citizens, brothers and sisters!

I address you, my friends, in a voice that might be my own, or perhaps that of someone before me.

You may feel that if we break from the continent above us, its enclosing plains of snow, we will disappear altogether from our corner of the world.

Fear not, my people. Those Soviets demanded too firm a hand; demanded to sit at our bedside with a cloth smothered heavily. Foreign to Stalin was my immovable brow. I, Tito, the only man to return his stare—racing back through his heart like mice.

While other leaders were busy believing everything about him, admiring him, it was I, comrades, who noticed the magnetism behind his eyes.

Fear not, my people. We have emerged from the fog of foreign occupation, watching dawn clear across the Balkans.

Onwards!

This morning the twilight is long in Belgrade, a drawn-out hour where the dogs and pigeons are still waking—moving more slowly than their shadows—as if our national character, anxious to rise earlier than usual, is weary from stirring through the night.

Tito takes breakfast quickly. On his way to his office he visits his canaries, feeds them, sings to them, sees to it that they have enough water, arriving early enough to catch dawn emptying its pockets. At his desk, he studies the morning papers. He reads in many languages—first, the Yugoslav papers in Cyrillic and Roman script, always turning to the letters to the editor. He then reads the London *Times*. In French, *Les Echos*. There is also *Neues Deutschland* and the Moscow Правда.

He reads fast, grasping immediately the most important facts. At first I would try to underline them before he arrived, so he'd know what was coming. 'Branko, you're a funny old Montenegrin,' he said to me. 'Don't you remember our time in the war? How I could see the snipers before each flash on the horizon?' Back then, Tito insisted on merely imitating the act of sleep in order to save time in the evenings. I remember his eyes half shut in the trenches, the pretend snoring, while his mind ticked over behind enemy lines. Now he is President and I ask him if the door should be left open or closed.

After the papers Tito attends to the mail. I am the first to open them: official reports, mostly, and government correspondence. Tito likes to oversee personally all matters regarding the state. There are also family letters. For instance, to encourage our women, it is now customary in Yugoslavia to name Tito as the godfather to every ninth born child. All of Tito's children lie in a pile on my desk. Tito their spiritual father, sending each on their wedding day a watch with no hands—a reminder of the work to be done.

Constitution of the Socialist Federal Republic of Yugoslavia, 1953

Article V: The Rights and Duties of Citizens

Section 37. The defence of the fatherland is the supreme duty and honour of every citizen. High treason is the greatest crime toward the people.

Section 38. No citizen is permitted to leave to a capitalist state. Anyone wishing to travel outside of these borders is complicit in waking from Yugoslavia's national dream. Our eternal dream. For there is nowhere to get to if you are already here.

Define *socialism* without using the words *social, labour, distribution, economic, theory,* or *equal.*

There was a folktale in Kotoriba about an old basket-maker named Andrija, famous in all of Međimurje for making the most detailed baskets one could imagine. Every autumn during the willow harvest, he would soak and dry his best strands for longer than usual, weaving a new design too beautiful to be carted away and sold. He kept these special baskets in a broom closet, safe from the eyes of all the other merchants, stacking them one on top of the other, year after year, until they spilled into the washroom, the sitting room. In the candlelight of his cottage, filling every corner, reaching up to every ceiling, beautiful wicker baskets.

Dear Marshal Tito,

Allow me to introduce myself. My name is Comrade ███████████ from ████████████████████.

Each day drags heavily by the scruff of the neck as we reap over and over the long strands of wheat. No matter how many steps we take, along the fields, the ration line (chips of beef fat, the stale bread we hide in our sleeves), it is only an illusion of movement.

I have held a scythe for so long my arms have taken on a life of their own, sharpening with each gesture. When I am not too tired, I think of inventions: grand ideas to propel my comrades into a new age of production. My dear Marshal, I must confess I have devised many failures (a mechanical duck, anti-drowning shoes), but I am writing to tell you that I have finally found the solution to what has plagued physicists for centuries. I have discovered the secret to perpetual motion.

The trick came to me in a dream. (I really should not be telling you, in case this letter is intercepted by another inventor, or worse, the Russians—in fact, I have not even told my wife.) All I will say is that it involves eight small metal balls, all of different weight, strung about on a string. My invention achieves what Da Vinci's and Drebbel's could not. Not even the Americans, with their air travel, their teams of researchers, could find the solution.

Just imagine, dear Marshal: speaking to a superior mind like yours, Yugoslavia could finally break the shackles of our Russian masters, those impregnable rogues, and secure herself as the superior Slavic race. The true oppressors are those who oppress the vigour of progress.

Dear leader, there is no time to be wasted. With winter coming, many of my comrades dream of crouching behind the haystacks to hide, unlike me, who now greets it with a raised fist. The unimagined life, after all, is a life not worth living.

Marshal Tito, you must come to ████████████████ at once!

Sincerely,

████████████

Characters

DOCTOR SORGA, cosmetic surgeon
MARSHAL TITO, Prime Minister of Yugoslavia
MARSHAL TITO, Body double of Prime Minister of
Yugoslavia

Act I

*1946, an unknown hospital of the State Security Administration,
Yugoslavia's secret police. Tito's body double lies asleep in a
hospital gown left of stage. A flickering light makes everything a
dull white: the concrete floor, the concrete walls, Tito's hardened
stare.*

DOCTOR and TITO *enter.*

DOCTOR [*inspecting the double's face*]: As you can see,
Marshal, he looks just like you. Strong jaw, a thinking brow—
your familiar stern expression, like he's evaluating the whole
world.

TITO: Very good.

DOCTOR: Our boys followed him for some time. One of
three. He even walked with the same direct gait, as if at all
times he had somewhere to get to.

DOCTOR *turns the page of his clipboard, marking it with a
pen.*

DOCTOR: And recovering as expected, I might add. He of course has not seen the things you have, Marshal, so we had to make him look slightly older than he is.

TITO: You flatter me, doctor. And his family?

DOCTOR: Gone. Not that he knows that. We've told him they're in Istria, or Austria, somewhere or another, where he will see them when all of this is done.

TITO: How long till we begin?

DOCTOR: About one year, Marshal. He will spend every day with Lojze Ljubiša, the actor who played you in *Partisans!* and *Operation Gvardijan*. He will study newsreels and film until our story is one hundred per cent accurate.

TITO *moves the sleeve of Tito's hospital gown, exposing the shoulder.*

TITO: My word, he even has the scar. A reminder of Sutjeska, an incident I can't quite place.

DOCTOR: Of course, Marshal, there can be no misstep! Think about it. Even the littlest of things, things that aren't necessarily noticed at first, they all come to add up somehow . . . Your hair, an unusually dark brown, for instance. Your Mediterranean tan. The way you stand so sure of yourself that you take up all of the space in the room. There's even the darkness underneath your eyes, two light thumbprints.

DOCTOR [*moving the double's sleeve back down*]: The resemblance will be so complete, even you yourself will have to strain for something to prove each other apart. A mole on your buttocks, say, or a forgotten taste of your mother's cooking. He will do more than merely look like you, act like you. He will of course become you.

DOCTOR *continues to make quiet scratches on his clipboard.*

DOCTOR: Whenever you're walking alone in the night, looking up at the sky with that feeling that only you and the moon are awake, listening to the sound of your footsteps, just remember there is a man out there exactly like you. Indeed, another you. A man you might cross in the street as if meeting your own reflection.

TITO: The public eye is always watching, comrade.

Belgrade 1947, days before the first unofficial Cominform meeting, Szklarska Poręba, Poland.

Tito briefs his body double for the first time. Both men stand in single-breasted military jackets. Tito's two canaries squabble back and forth in their cage left of stage, speaking in several languages.

TITO: You will only travel at night, or behind tinted windows, always showing up at the perfect moment—right as things begin.

TITO: Yes, Marshal.

TITO: No one is to question you.

TITO: No, Marshal.

TITO: Even when you're speaking to the most imposing figures of our time—Rákosi, Hoxha, even Stalin, who makes everyone in his presence feel like a boy—you must never hesitate.

TITO: Yes, Marshal.

TITO [*looking away, as he has all year, unable to meet his double's eye*]: Last night I dreamt of a train crash.

TITO: You did?

TITO: It reminded me of the war. Shrapnel, the sound of bayonet to bone.

TITO *claps hands!*

TITO: Can you imagine it? This very evening, Serbia to Szklarska! With every click, my heart skipping *at once at once.*

TITO *smoothes the sides of his jacket before pacing the room.*

TITO: You will go in my place. Shake hands, perhaps a toast. I will arrive by motor car without the fanfare of photographers and foreign dignitaries.

TITO [*removing his wig, revealing an identical haircut underneath*]: As you wish, Marshal.

TITO: One day I will build my own locomotive. A beautiful blue train, with soft blue carpets, blue silk and velvet. My cook will serve mushrooms, pickled garlic, berries and bleu de Bresse. We'll shake off the last of the seaside villages dotted along the coastline, towards an Adriatic spilling into the open Mediterranean.

IV: Stjepan

In the afternoon, past the fields,
looking for something to take us beyond
the rows and rows of clustered bean stalks.
Nettles, perhaps. Snapping the bony fingers
off trees. We lead into the wood
with a century of weapons over our shoulders—
flashing imaginary swords and rifles:
Croatians going one way, Hungarians the other.
With rocks that pierce the green skin
of the Mura, which flows over the border,
below the rolled-up trousers
of other boys in their own history.

Constitution of the Socialist Federal Republic of Yugoslavia, 1953

Article V: The Rights and Duties of Citizens

Section 30. The privacy of letters and other means of communication is inviolable except in cases of criminal inquiry.

Section 31. [Line is missing]

Section 32. [Line is crossed out]

Section 33. Military service is universal for all men.

My majka once heard a man beg for his life.
The sky had no stars then, she remembered.
They had walked for days, barefoot,
fleeing the Hungarians.

We sat at the table around a single candle.
My baka with her soiled playing cards,
us children practising our spelling and counting.
Majka pinched her fingers

to thread the eye of a needle, patching
and repatching her hopes over our trousers.
'I could hear his voice breaking,' she said,
'over the crunch of dead leaves.'

As cadets we were taught to count
the rings of freshly cut trees,
to tread our soles without squeaking.

1. Most Sundays, when the light was bleeding in through the glass, I wanted to ask if he actually looked like that, ascending.
2. At communion, Majka told me to dip the bread instead of drinking, because of the germs.
3. I still didn't know the Oče Naŝ by heart.

'At first we thought they were just distant rocks starting to show, perhaps birds?' My stric often told us these stories from the war. This time, the Carpathians, after both sides had retreated from the cold.

'We were coming down the mountains slowly. Snow was thawing across the battlefields, enough that the hands of dead soldiers could be seen reaching upwards.'

He paused to fill his pipe.

'I'd never seen anything like it, on both sides of the road, crossing field after white field:

hundreds, thousands of hands
reaching out to greet us.'

A trick, sister:

hold the chicken upside down
softly so as not to break the twigs of its legs,
firmly enough not to alarm the heart, and then,
with your other arm, bring the bird to your chest
as you would an infant, calming its wings—
pressing it harder and harder against you
until, eyes fluttering, it stiffens into sleep. And it is only then
that it will stay there for some moments, still,
this chicken, as if frozen,
lying upside down,
lifelessly twitching its feet
toward the ceiling.

'Forgive me, dear, for his voice is weary from the distance
between worlds,' the old gypsy would say.

This woman from the neighbouring village,
who foretold to majkas

during the war
which of their sons would return.

Majkas came from all over Medjimurje
just to see her

make the sign of the cross,
to feel in her hands the emptiness

of a whole generation.
No one questioned her.

Outside, silence
bristled like a cat

as the rest of the village
looked on.

In my eighteenth year I was to join the army.
My tata had given me a cut-throat razor,
my majka, a book she'd strung together by hand.
She told me that the pages scared her, the empty space
only I could fill.

V: The Company We Keep

i.   History has never been an exact science. It is simply an
     emphasis of fact: figures moving in and out of view with
     a preoccupied smoothness, the way dates and events go
     missing like memories treading just above the surface.
ii. One cannot be certain of anything except for what one
     sees with one's own eyes.

1.   A forgotten birth

1.1 It was Tito himself who started the confusion about his
     birth. All Yugoslavs celebrate his birthday on 25 May,
     but some say this is really a testament to our collective
     forgetfulness—that the exact date is unknown. That
     even his team of biographers and party members, his
     own mother, aren't in on the secret.

1.2 Officially, Tito had the simplest of upbringings:
     christened Josip Broz, the seventh of eight peasant
     children of Franjo, a Croat, and Marija, a Slovene. His
     birth house, built in 1860, was the first brickwork house
     in the village.

1.3 And to most, 1892 was simply a year like any other: a
     few things beginning, a few things coming to an end.
     Yugoslavia was still twenty-six years from its inception.

1.4 Count Dragutin was Ban of the Kingdom of Croatia-
     Slavonia (as these lands were known then). His reign
     is remembered as the *khuenovština*—twenty years of
     restraint, like a blindfold pulled too tightly, leaving sharp
     marks under the eyes. Only the year before, in 1891,
     was Dragutin awarded the Order of the Golden Fleece,

one of the most prestigious orders of chivalry in Europe. Such figures as Louis XVIII, Napoleon, and Isabella II of Spain hung the little gold badge at their breasts.

1.5　Tito was conceived somewhere along the Podsreda ranges on a journey home from Ljubljana. Ripples of this story surfaced many years later. In fact, during his inauguration speech in 1953, the President instructed all young newlyweds to rush high into the wilderness, so that an entire generation of Yugoslavs would begin in this world, like him, at an elevated origin.

1.6　In 1892, there were of course many other important births. We cannot forget it was the year Ivo Andrić entered the world, the great Bosnian writer—the first and only Yugoslav to win the Nobel Prize for Literature. There was also the dashing Croatian actor Tito Strozzi (the second most famous Tito in Yugoslavia). Manfred von Richthofen, better known as the *Crveni Barun* (in English, the Red Baron), too decided to begin his short life making beautiful allied graves. Even Andrei Yeremenko, Tito's counterpart, the Marshal of the Soviet Union, was born that very year.

2.　A second look

2.1　An old folktale in Yugoslavia goes that while a Josip Broz was born in Kumrovec on 25 March 1892, this wasn't really the Josip Broz we all think of. This man, the real Josip Broz it was claimed, was in fact killed in April 1915 somewhere in the Carpathians. This Josip was a soldier, like Tito, of the Habsburg Army.

2.2   All records of this man (photographs, papers, letters
       home in the war) are said to be kept in some small, dark
       drawer in Belgrade.

2.3   Some, too, have noted Tito's strange accent. A
       strangeness noticeable only to native speakers of the
       Krapina-Zagorje district. How his Serbo-Croatian,
       while flawless, catches slightly over some consonants as
       a foreigner's would. As if, while forming the words with
       his tongue in all his consideration, the natural sound
       was lost before reaching his lips. For some reason there
       is a faint strain to it. But who would ever notice that? A
       peasant from Kumrovec, fluent in Russian and German,
       fumbling over his own mother-tongue?

3.   Josip as Tito
3.1   Josip Broz used 'Tito' as a pseudonym when writing
       articles for party journals in 1934. He was first officially
       documented as 'Tito' that same year, in the minutes of a
       Central Committee meeting.

3.2   In the 1930s, many Communist Party members were
       known by nicknames. Tito himself explains that
       'during those uncertain days, it was Party policy to
       never under any circumstances go by one's birth name.
       Arrests were often, but even after removing our teeth,
       toenails, the police would never find us behind our
       invented selves.'

3.3   Of course, even these invented names often had to be
       changed. Broz went by many others, such as 'Walter'

(in the Comintern), 'Rudi', 'Timo', 'Oto' and 'Ivan Kostanjšek', so as always to stay one step ahead.

3.4   The great eighteenth-century playwright and poet Tituš Brezovački, a father of Slavic literature, was also known as Tito. As was the Yugoslav novelist Ksaver Šandor Gjalski, whose birth name was Ljubomil Tito Josip Franjo Babić.

3.5   Tito was known to travel with a forged Swedish passport, assuming the name 'John Alexander Karlsson'. He also possessed a Canadian passport, in the name of 'Spiridon Mekas'.

3.6   In an interview with *Life* magazine, Broz revealed that he simply adopted the name Tito as it was 'common in his native Zagorje region' and had 'no special meaning'.

Characters

MARSHAL TITO, Prime Minister of Yugoslavia
DRAŽA MIHAILOVIĆ, Leader of the Chetniks
Detachments of the Yugoslav Army

Act IV: A Dream

1946. Evening, Office of Prime Minister. Centre stage is a chair and large oak desk. Tito is sitting cross-legged, flicking his cigarette-holder into an ashtray, as is his habit when working late in the night.

MIHAILOVIĆ *enters.*

TITO [*without lifting his eyes from his papers*]: You're exactly the person I wanted to see.

MIHAILOVIĆ: Is that so, Marshal?

TITO: Exactly.

MIHAILOVIĆ: Exactly?

TITO *puts his cigarette down then picks it up immediately.*

TITO: Exactly. It's as if you know everything and nothing, Draža.

MIHAILOVIĆ: You called for me, Marshal?

TITO: Are you sure of that, Draža?

MIHAILOVIĆ *shifts his weight, touching the knot of his tie.*

MIHAILOVIĆ [*clearing his throat*]: I, I am. Branko came past my door on the way out, pointing a light hand. The rap of his knuckles sounded like feet.

TITO: Perhaps that is how you remember it just now. But perhaps you are mistaken? Perhaps it was you who in fact called for me?

MIHAILOVIĆ: Marshal?

TITO: Sit down, my friend.

White knots of smoke linger in the air. The light from Tito's lamp holds the glow of each expression on his calm, fixed face.

MIHAILOVIĆ *sits.*

[remainder of the page is missing]

MIHAILOVIĆ: And sir, before I rattle home on the tram, may I ask for Branko to order more of that South American coffee, for I have not been sleeping.

TITO: Others are not sleeping either.

MIHAILOVIĆ [*looking down*]: The list is long, sir.

TITO: List? Why, they should be thankful. For there is no greater relief than a midnight knock at the door. In fact, they should even *want* to be woken, for once you're held you have nothing left to fear.

MIHAILOVIĆ: Marshal?

TITO: Don't you see, Draža? When everyone around you is being hauled off by blindfold, never to be seen again, and they—our boys in double-breasted black suits, their gold lapels—have not yet come. For some reason they have decided to spend another day rearranging your shoes. For some reason they are taking their time.

TITO *moves some papers on his desk, clinking his typewriter to the left of the margin.*

MIHAILOVIĆ: It's late, sir.

TITO: They say, Draža, that when a man is about to suffocate, when he finally let's go of the wire around his neck, it's actually relieving for a moment. A final surge in the mind before it loses its grip on the world.

MIHAILOVIĆ: I really should be going.

TITO *stares at the small cards pinned to the wall, as if looking through them.*

TITO: You're exactly the person I wanted to see, Draža.

DEPARTMENT OF THE NATIONAL LIBRARY,
SOCIALIST FEDERAL REPUBLIC OF YUGOSLAVIA

Present this card when borrowing books

No..........**0-772**..........................

Expires............**Jul. 1955**...........

Tito, Josip Broz.
15 Užička Street, Belgrade, Serbia

In an interview with the European New York Times, *Tito was asked to name books he had issued from the National Library. Each title has caused much speculation.*

THE ART OF ORATORY
(New York, The Century Co., 1936)

Looking over my shoulder so often,
a team of surgeons permanently fixed my head backwards.
During speeches, I now wear a suit back to front,
my tie always slightly crooked from having to reach behind me.
If you don't believe me, spot
my heels beneath the lectern, firmly planted
a shoulder-width apart.

JACQUES-LOUIS DAVID: A LIFE
(Genève, Albert Skira 1908)

'The political death is the most painful
of all deaths,' David says, as he and I
rob graves. Him, for the corpses of radical Jacobins,
me, Yugoslav generals who buried themselves alive.

Our fingernails are blackened from the soil,
as he tells me his theories on the anatomical soul:
how 'to give a body and a perfect form to one's thought',
for example, 'this—and only this—is to be an artist'.

It's illegal to dig up old bones
in this way, but we have to be sure their hearts
are no longer beating, to study the circulation of dissent,
the way cartilage and vessels are shaped

towards a certain cause.
At dawn, one of us paints flowers
at the foot of a gravestone, the other
a cadaver with the expression of a breathing man.

INFECTIOUS DIVIDES: PERSPECTIVES ON
MODERN MEDICINE
(Boston, Beacon Press, 1949)

Enunciate as if you've swallowed a tray of scalpels,
marking each incision of speech clearly, calmly,
all the way to the bone.

I could've been a surgeon in a past life,
sterilising blades in my solitude
and through a stethoscope, listening to the restlessness
of blood.

The effort of conspiracy is always preventable.
I can see it in their eyes, the unrefreshed stare
of men who toss and turn
in the night.

With steady hands, my assistant
holds each tongue as he would
a postage stamp.

THE COMPANY WE KEEP: A PLAY IN FIVE PARTS
(St. Petersburg, Znanie, 1898)

Am I still leader?
Blackness, sacks over their heads
        in the middle of the night.
So late it's early. Frost,
the collective drawing of breath.

LOST TENDENCIES: PORTRAITS OF YUGOSLAVIA
(Belgrade City Museum, 1957)

The first painting in my gallery
of dreams: a canvas the colour of factory smoke.
I stand patiently where I shouldn't be
in front of a long red rope, admiring the works
of Yugoslav grand masters
scampering out of their frames:
faces of peasants passing through from a funeral,
an unknown woman searching for a quiet place to pose.
Even a medieval Christ removes his hands
one nail at a time, asking for a cigarette and some clothes,
dripping petals of blood onto the marble floor.
I hear myself shouting at him across the foyer,
its endless distance, in a language I don't understand—Aramaic—
consternation, perhaps?

THE PSYCHOPATHOLOGY OF EVERYDAY LIFE
(New York, The Macmillan Company, 1914)

Tito was ill and missed the first speech
delivered by his double. He listened to it
on the radio like everyone else.

His new self feels like he's always having to explain himself,
memorising so many platitudes for Tito to forget
the next day that it's hard to know
if his double is now thinking like Tito, or if
Tito is doing the thinking for him.

Only last week he fumbled his lines during a speech
only to remember that no one around him had any idea whom
they were actually listening to.

There's nothing more rapturous than moving a crowd
of countrymen, he decides,
an entire race together in their applause.
The two canaries in the next room agree. One takes off its mask,
revealing itself to be the other one all along.

THE HISTORY OF THE NECKTIE
(London, Penguin, 1925)

A mark of remembrance, the women thought,
wrapping thin bands of cloth around their husband's necks,
so they'd look handsome
when being stabbed to death by the Prussians.
In 1636, the first of the Croatian mercenaries rode West.
'More like the Three Hundred Years' War,' said their wives,
waiting nervously for them to return,
imagining how they looked in uniform
before Louis XIII at the steps of Versailles—
each one proudly displaying the colours
of their wife's eyes, wrapped once
around the neck, then twice.

VI: Elizabeta's Tiny Seeds

I was never disloyal to him.
As a child, if someone shared a bad thought
I would cover my ears, suppress it,
continue on with my devotion.

Inside the barn, where the farmers hide crops
from the authorities, it is so quiet
even the mice become scared of their footsteps.
All alone between the walls, they forget to scurry
under the haystacks for potatoes, corn,
as if they can hear the trucks approaching;
the sound of heavy boots pausing at the door.
The cockroaches sit on an empty milk crate to play chess.
'These secrets are safe with me,' one says
as he nibbles on a knight's ear, once again
mistaking it for food.

The dead farmer wanders out of his grave.
At first, it's hard to tell him apart from the others,
this thin-faced man, carrying his own rib bones in his hands;
his naked legs following the lines of the soil.
He's come to check on his tomatoes, blackened by frost,
as if, after all this time, the skins might've unburned themselves.
'I knew this would happen,' he says to his widowed wife,
who offers him a shot of rakija before he goes,
back to tell the others buried beyond the wood.

An old woman washing clothes on the Mura:
Why would you question that? she asks.
She knows everything about the flat rocks at the river's edge,
the washed sky, at first foggy then red—the sun slipping
through its own lining. I watch her every movement,
rinsing and wringing, rinsing again. If I look away
I won't have to imagine who will wear them—
the same family story—
or if she is retrieving
the stray handkerchief floating downstream,
set free from its basket
          like a piece of torn cloud.

A tiny seed of doubt. How dissatisfaction and stillness for years thicken one another. Probably I would've gone back to life in the fields, the same rows of dirt in the beating sun, if he had not forgotten us here on the Hungarian border.

With each mechanical address, speaking as a veteran, about how all Yugoslav sons would repeat his steps in marching formation, Tito's image started to retreat to another part of my mind, not completely out of sight, but no longer in its continual foreground.

In my dreams Stjepan walked with me, hand in hand past the wood, where there was something beyond not quite of this world, too big to hold in the sleeve of my shirt.

Before they came to take him, I told my brother a story about our ancestors. How some Slavic women, centuries ago, went to war with their husbands and brothers. 'Even in 626,' I said, 'at the siege of Constantinople, the Greeks found hundreds of female bodies among the dead Slavs.'

His gold buttons, the way they shone in a straight line before him. A military-issued pocket mirror, the thick woollen lining of his greatcoat, a distance between us.

We stood there without speaking. The morning spread heavily, the hills forgetting which way to cast their shadows across the plains.

Could it possibly be the same blue
as my dreams? The sea he would finally find.
When we were children, my majka once took us to a lake
and we begged her to tell us about the stillness.
'The same blue as the sky,' she told us, 'only different.'
Like mushrooms darkening
in a pot. The way different qualities of light
make birds fear they are flying
in the wrong direction.

Our small railway station, where the whole village trembles
with the thought of being shrugged away—
children shouted names
over the low, rumbling engine. My last image of him:
Stjepan's face through the glass compartment
blurred white by the morning glare.

One relative in Zagreb who is now missing (the flick of a torch, blindfold) once asked if Tito was really who he said he was. Most of the diaries were burned or fell to the hand of the censor. Odd details, however, evaded detection:

1. 14 Sep. 1945
   This allied victory will cut his life in two: his fifty-two years as an outlaw, living in the shadows of secret meeting rooms and false identities, and the beginning of his national fatherhood.

2. 7 Jun. 1946
   Bloody Secret Police! His way to observe every movement of our people, to see things before they happen.

3. 9 Aug. 1946
   T is a hungry man and I suppose this is why we adore him.

It was Tito, after all, who taught us the habit of looking out at the world, then back to our wobbling corner of Europe, where everything was destined to happen.

VII: Escape

I'd heard stories from the other side—
ghosts of bakas coming back
to haunt those seeking to leave;
the sound of frail hands wringing the necks
of chickens.

Sometimes I'm not sure if Kotoriba was ever really there:
its straw roofs and dirt roads, the Mura River, day after day
the ration line shuffling
out of sight.

I left in the dark, when the farmers had stopped singing.
I hid under a pile of dirty potatoes
all the way to the Slovenian border.
I had partisans in the family. I thought of their voices
the next morning, coarse
from cursing, as my boots brushed through the bushes.
Fallen leaves.
The dark boughs deepening
around me.

A trick, sister:

It is said that Yugoslavian-made maps
have intentionally false borders,
tracing the corners of neighbours
like the black lines of a forged signature
so accurate that you begin to question
your own name.

When you leave for good,
guards wait in invented towns.
Some climb trees, others patrol the hills
and roads that lead to nowhere in particular.
Night falls.

The lines you do not see

mark the snake's skin beneath the grass.

The alps were filled with echoes:
the sound of their footsteps slowing,
like drips catching in a pot—
as if there was always someone approaching,
or just moving away.

I ate frost to hide my breath.
My eyes became used to the darkness,
the thread of barbed wire glinting along the trees.

For a moment I heard the hungry murmurs
of the guards inside. An opening—
forgetting their cups on the bench, the rattle of cards and coins—
as I turned my back on Maribor,
its lights, its flickering teeth.

At first it didn't seem any different.
The same needled larch trees.
Children passing along the river
to school.

I sat in my ripped stockings
and ate something similar to ćevapčići,
while the alps hurried off
somewhere behind me.

After breakfast I reported myself
to the Austrian authorities.
Without papers, a passport,
the balding official

suspected I only existed
in my own head:
another of Tito's children
in the end.

Lyall Bay, 1959

The evening sharpens. A light which takes hold of the day, puts everything back when it's finished—a different order. Crisp air. My lungs. How low the sky is. How low? The night is coming.

Trees moan. The sound of ghosts, sleepless women. The hills, a creased jacket on the horizon.

Words circle above the surface, like birds. Not quite speech. Something forgotten. An entire country lost in thought.

My feet heavy. Streetlights. Threads of light. Not even he could follow me here. Or could he? His footsteps. Do I hear them just now?

Darkness knits over the holes, my hands. The distances between—a different hue are my murmurs of the past.

How it stretches out before me. Too big to carry. Memory. My shadow unpins itself from my body and wanders off into the night.

I have walked alone from the other end. To a house, its eyes. Its red roof, as if drawn by a child.

The sea reaching against it, reaching again. A wash of colour. My hairs stand on their ends. A kind of winter passing through the water.

Chronology

1892 Josip Broz is born in Kumrovec, Kingdom of Croatia-Slavonia, Austro-Hungarian Empire.

1914 At twenty-one, Josip Broz becomes the youngest officer in Austro-Hungarian Army.

1918 Balkan Slavic states are united as the Kingdom of Serbs, Croats and Slovenes.

1919 Josip Broz joins the Communist Party of Yugoslavia, at the time an illegal underground group.

1929 Kingdom of Serbs, Croats and Slovenes becomes Kingdom of Yugoslavia.

1934 Josip Broz adopts the name Tito.

1934 King Alexander I of Yugoslavia, known as Alexander the Unifier, is assassinated in Marseilles.

1941 Kingdom of Yugoslavia is invaded by Nazi Germany.

1943 Tito becomes Marshal of Yugoslavia, the supreme commander of the Yugoslav People's Army.

1945 Tito is appointed Prime Minister of Yugoslavia.

1946 Yugoslavia's socialist government enforce agricultural collectivisation. The State Security Administration, Yugoslavia's secret police, is formed in March.

1953 Tito appoints himself President (later President for Life). Under a revised constitution, it becomes illegal for Yugoslav citizens to leave Yugoslavia for a capitalist state.

Notes

The epigraphs on p. 8 are from Joseph Conrad's *Under Western Eyes* (first published 1911; London: Methuen, 1948), p. 7; and Ivo Andrić's 'The Story of the Vizier's Elephant' (first published 1947), translated by Celia Hawkesworth, in *The Damned Yard and Other Stories*, edited by Celia Hawkesworth (Beograd: Dereta, 2007), p. 25.

A number of historical sources have been quoted in this book. Tito's letter to Stalin is quoted from Robert Service's *Stalin: A Biography* (London: Macmillan, 2004), p. 592.

The line 'All were obliged to guess the temperature outside and drink a glass of vodka for every degree they were out' on p. 13 is taken from Richard West, *Tito and the Rise and Fall of Yugoslavia* (London: Faber & Faber, 2012), p. 224.

The line 'and not the solution of Stalin' is an idea from Lloyd Jones's *Biografi* (Wellington: VUP, 1993), p. 93.

Two quotes on p. 26 are from Ivo Andrić's *The Bridge on the Drina* (1959), translated by Lovett F. Edwards (Chicago: University of Chicago Press, 1977).

Two quotes on p. 27 are from Josip Smodlaka's *Yugoslav Territorial Claims Lecture* (1919), quoted in Dejan Djokić's *Pašić and Trumbić: The Kingdowm of Serbs, Croats and Slovenes* (London: Haus Publishing, 2010), pp. 4–5.

Some details of Tito's morning routine on p. 33 are taken from Vladimir Dedijer's *Tito Speaks: His Self Portrait and Struggle with Stalin* (London: Weidenfeld and Nicolson, 1953), p. 420.

While mostly invented, parts of pp. 34 and 46 are quoted directly from the official Yugoslav Constitution of 1953.

Some quotes from the historical sequence (pp. 57–60) were sourced from: Dedijer's *Tito Speaks*, pp. 125–6; an article on History.info titled '1934: Joship Broz Takes the Nickname "Tito"' (history.info/on-this-day/1934-josip-broz-takes-the-nickname-tito/) and 'Tito Speaks Part II', *Life* magazine, 28 April 1952, p. 69.

On p. 67, the quote 'To give a body and a perfect form to one's thought, this—and only this—is to be an artist' is from Jacques-Louis David (1796), in *Artists on Art, from the XIV to the XX Century*, third ed. 1974, translated by Marco Treves, edited by Robert Goldwater (New York: Pantheon Books), p. 206.

On p. 80, the line 'the Greeks found hundreds of female bodies among the dead Slavs' is from the Russian historian Nikolai Karamzin, quoted in Svetlana Alexievich's *The Unwomanly Face of War* (1985), translated by Richard Pevear and Larissa Volokhonsky (London: Penguin, 2017), p. 1.

Glossary

baka: grandmother
ćevapčići: a grilled dish of minced meat
majka: mother
Oče Naŝ: The Lord's Prayer
stric: paternal uncle
tata: father

Acknowledgements

Thank you to my majka and deda, who as teenagers escaped communist Yugoslavia in 1957 and whose story inspired much of this book.

I'm indebted to everyone who read my early drafts during my MA year at the IIML. Thank you to James Brown, Chris Price and my classmates: Alie Benge, Anna Rankin, the real Catherine Russ, Charlotte Forester, Glenda Lewis, Madison Hamill, Rose Lu and Susanne Jungerson. Cheers to James Pasley as well. Thanks of course to the Holly Hunter Memorial Writing Group of Barnaby McIntosh, Ella Borrie, Emma Hurley, Holly Hunter and Jayne Iris Mulligan. I'm also very grateful to Peter and Mary Biggs for their generosity and warm hospitality over the years.

Ashleigh Young's editorial advice was essential to the arrival of this book. As was the work from the wider VUP team of Fergus Barrowman, Kirsten McDougall and Tayi Tibble.

Thanks also to Todd Atticus for the cover and to Ebony Lamb for the author photo.

Special mention goes to my dad who unknowingly took the back cover photo on a trip to Kotoriba in 1980 and to my brother Petar.

Most importantly, thank you to my partner Issey for her patience.